CAMP FIRE GIRLS

THE HAND SIGN OF CAMP FIRE

This photograph illustrates the abbreviated hand sign, used as a
private signal. (See page 4 for the complete signal.)

CAMP FIRE GIRLS
(of America)

PUBLISHED FOR

THE CAMP FIRE GIRLS

118 EAST 28TH STREET, NEW YORK

APPLEWOOD BOOKS
Carlisle, Massachusetts

Camp Fire Girls
was originally published in 1912.

Copyright by Luther Halsey Gulick

ISBN 978-1-4290-9103-9

For a free copy of our current print catalog featuring our bestselling books, write to:

APPLEWOOD BOOKS
P.O. Box 27
Carlisle, MA 01741

For more complete listings,
visit us on the web at:
www.awb.com

" Burn, fire, burn!
Flicker, flicker, flame!
Whose hand above this blaze is lifted
Shall be with magic touch engifted,
To warm the hearts of lonely mortals
Who stand without their open portals.
The torch shall draw them to the fire
Higher, higher
By desire.
Whoso shall stand by this hearthstone,
Flame-fanned,
Shall never, never stand alone;
Whose house is dark and bare and cold,
Whose house is cold,
This is his own.
Flicker, flicker, flicker, flame.
Burn, fire, burn! "

COUNCIL

COMMITTEE ON ORGANIZATION

CAMP FIRE GIRLS

THE LAW OF THE CAMP FIRE GIRLS

Seek beauty
Give service
Pursue knowledge
Be trustworthy
Hold on to health
Glorify work
Be happy

Name.— This organization shall be known as the Camp Fire Girls. Each local group should have some special name. To show the relationship to the nation-wide movement it is desirable, although not necessary, that each local name have the words "Camp Fire" in its title — e. g., "Hudson River Camp Fire," "Albany Camp Fire," "Aloha Camp Fire," "Vala Camp Fire," etc.

Object.— The object is to add the power of organization and the charm of romance to health, work, and play.

Membership.— Any girl who meets the tests for membership may become a Camp Fire Girl. A member becomes, first, a Wood Gatherer; second, a Fire Maker; third, a Torch Bearer.

3

Symbols and Signs.— The symbol is Fire. For purposes of decoration the fire symbol may be indicated by the rising sun.

The symbol of membership is the standing pine. It means simplicity and strength.

The watch words are, Work, Health, and Love. The first two letters of each of the words are combined so as to create the special word Wohelo for general use.

The hand sign, which comes from the sign language of the early American Indian, is made by flattening the fingers of the right hand against those of the left. This indicates crossed wood. From this position the right hand is raised, following the curves of an imaginary flame. The sign is abbreviated (see frontispiece) when it is necessary to use a private or inconspicuous signal. At such times the fingers of the right hand are placed across those of the left, with the forefinger of the right hand slightly raised.

Local Camp Fires. — Each local group shall be called a Camp Fire. Experience has shown that a local Camp Fire should be composed of from six to twenty girls — from ten to twelve in number is the most desirable. It is best to have the girls in each Camp Fire of about the same degree of maturity, for this enables them to work together easily.

Meetings. — There shall be regular weekly meetings of the local Camp Fire. The Council Fire is the monthly ceremonial meeting of a Camp Fire at which all regular business, admission of members and distribution of honors take place.

Guardian. — The head of a Camp Fire shall be called the Guardian of the Fire. In age, character, and attainment she must be a woman who is suitable as a leader. Every

Guardian shall have received, before organizing a group, a Certificate of Authorization. Application forms for such certificates can be secured from National Headquarters. In communities where there is an Adviser the application must be accompanied by the Adviser's endorsement.

Chief Guardian. — A Chief Guardian is the official head of a group of local Camp Fires all within one organization — i. e., Playground Association, Young Women's Christian Association, etc.

Adviser or Advisory Board. — In large cities, or where there are a number of Camp Fires, there may be an Adviser or an Advisory Board, who shall supervise the work of the Guardians. In a city thus organized the ranking officers are: Advisory Board or Adviser, Chief Guardian and Guardian.

TESTS FOR MEMBERSHIP AND RANK

WOOD GATHERER

THE WOOD GATHERER'S DESIRE

It is my desire to become a Camp Fire Girl, and to obey the Law of the Camp Fire, which is to

> Seek beauty
> Give service
> Pursue knowledge
> Be trustworthy
> Hold on to health
> Glorify work
> Be happy:

This Law of the Camp Fire I will strive to follow.

To become a Wood Gatherer

The applicant must know the object and requirements of the organization, and at the monthly meeting of the Council Fire shall announce her decision to become a Camp Fire Girl by repeating the Wood Gatherer's Desire.

The Guardian explains the Law, phrase by phrase; then standing before the Guardian of the Fire the candidate repeats the Wood Gatherer's desire and is taught the Sign.

6

FIRE MAKER

THE FIRE MAKER'S DESIRE

As fuel is brought to the fire
So I purpose to bring
My strength
My ambition
My heart's desire
My joy
And my sorrow
To the fire
Of humankind
For I will tend
As my fathers have tended
And my fathers' fathers
Since time began
The fire that is called
The love of man for man
The love of man for God.

To become a Fire Maker

1. The candidate must have been a Wood Gatherer for not less than three months unless she is living under such conditions as to permit her to give her entire time to preparation — as for example at camp. Under these conditions one month may be accepted.

2. The candidate shall further indicate her love and understanding of the Camp Fire ideal by learning and repeating the Fire Maker's Desire.

3. Other requirements are:

(1) *a.* To help prepare and serve, together with the other candidates, at least two meals for meetings of the Camp Fire; this is to include purchase of food, cooking and serving the meal, and care of fire. (All candidates work in rotation; that is, each does a different part of the work each time.) *b.* Two meals prepared in the home without advice or help may be substituted.

(2) To mend a pair of stockings, a knitted undergarment and hem a dish towel.

(3) To keep a written classified account of all money received and spent for at least one month.

(4) To tie a square knot five times in succession correctly and without hesitation.

(5) To sleep with open windows or out of doors for at least one month.

(6) To take an average of at least half an hour daily outdoor exercise for not less than a month.

(7) To refrain from sodas and candy between meals for at least one month.

(8) To name the chief causes of infant mortality in summer. Tell how and to what extent it has been reduced in one American community.

(9) To know what to do in the following emergencies:

      a. Clothing on fire.

      b. Person in deep water who cannot swim, both in summer and through ice in winter.

      c. Open cut.

      d. Frosted foot.

      e. Fainting.

(10) To know the principles of elementary bandaging and how to use surgeon's plaster.

(11) To know what a girl of her age needs to know about herself.

(12) To commit to memory any good poem or song not less than twenty-five lines in length.

(13) To know the career of some woman who has done much for the country or state.

(14) To know and sing all the words of My Country 'Tis of Thee.

4. In addition the candidate shall present twenty Elective Honors (see pages 10–16). At least one honor must be won in each group and with the exception of Home Craft not more than five honors may be presented from any one group.

TORCH BEARER

THE TORCH BEARER'S DESIRE

That light which has been given to me,
I desire to pass undimmed to others.

A Torch Bearer is an assistant to the Guardian. She is a leader. That is what carrying the torch means.

To become a Torch Bearer.

1. The candidate shall have been a Fire Maker in good standing for three months, unless she has been able to give her entire time to preparation, as in camp. In the latter case one month may be accepted.

2. The candidate shall learn and repeat the Torch Bearer's Desire.

3. The candidate must be known to the Guardian as trust-

worthy, happy, unselfish, a good leader, a good "team worker,'
and as liked by the other girls.

4. The candidate shall have organized a group of not less
than three girls and led them regularly in any of the Camp
Fire activities for not less than three months, or one month if
she gives her entire time as in camp. The real test is the
enthusiasm and success of the girls she teaches.

5. The candidate shall present fifteen honors from the list
of Elective Honors in addition to those she presented for the
rank of Fire Maker.

ELECTIVE HONORS

The number of stars indicates the number of honors which may be won under a given heading; e. g.:

* indicates one honor.

**** indicate four honors.

HEALTH CRAFT

First Aid: Secure diploma of the American Red Cross, or joint diploma of the American Red Cross and of the Young Women's Christian Association.*

Colds: Be free from colds for two consecutive months between October and April.*

Regularity: Not miss work or school because of ill health or headaches for three consecutive months.*

Diet: Abstain from candy and sodas between meals for three months.*

Sleep: Sleep out of doors or with wide open windows for two consecutive months between October and April.*

Games: Play any of the following games for not less than fifteen hours in any one month.* *Team Games* — Hockey, Volley Ball, Basketball, Baseball, Soccer, Prisoner's Base, Captain Ball. *Other Games* — Tennis, Golf, Run Sheep Run, Hide and Seek, Pussy Wants a Corner, Three Deep, Blind Man's Buff, Tie the Handkerchief, Red Rover, Fox and Hounds, Quoits, Duck on the Rock.

Swimming: Swim one hundred yards.*

Swim one mile *in any six days.* (Not necessarily consecutive.) *

Fetch up a cup from the bottom in eight feet of water. *

Do any two standard dives in good form.*

Standard Dives:

Standing — Front, Side Back Twist, Jack.

Running or from spring board the same, e. g., a standing front and a running front and a front from a run and use of spring board may all be presented.

Undress in deep water.*

Swim any four standard styles.*

Standard styles are breast, side, over-hand single over-hand, crawl, back, scull on back, etc.

Canoe or Boat: Paddle or row twenty miles *in any five days.* (Not necessarily consecutive.)*

Sailing: Sail a boat without help or advice for fifty miles.* (In any one season.)

Motor Boat: Operate and care for without help or advice for one hundred miles.* (In any one season.)

Skating — Ice or Roller: Skate twenty-five miles *in any five days.** (Not necessarily consecutive.)*

Bicycle: Bicycle forty miles *in any five days.* (Not necessarily consecutive.)* Know how to make minor repairs on bicycle.*

Horseback: Ride forty miles in any five days.* (Not necessarily consecutive.) Take care of horse and stable for at least one month.*

Mountain Climbing: Make an ascent of two thousand feet and return to the starting level.*

Snowshoeing: Cover twenty-five miles *in any five days.* (Not necessarily consecutive.)*

Tramping: Walk forty miles in any ten days.* (Not necessarily consecutive.) Note: This means tramping in the country or walking to and from school or business.

Automobile: Operate and care for without help or advice, for five hundred miles.* (In any one season.)

Folk Dancing: Know any five standard folk dances.*

HOME CRAFT

Cooking: Make bread in two ways and two kinds of cake.*
Make ten standard soups.*
Cook meat in four ways: Roast, broil, fricassee, boil.*
Cook left-over meats in four ways.*
Cook three common vegetables each in three ways.*
Prepare six salads.*
Gather two quarts of wild berries or fruits and make them into a dessert.*
Can or preserve three different kinds of fruits, at least one quart of each kind.*
Invalid cookery: Prepare two kinds of gruel, eggs in four suitable ways, milk toast, and to arrange a tray attractively.*
Chafing dish: Prepare six unconventional appetizing dishes.*
Plan an appetizing balanced vegetarian diet for a week.*
Compare energy and tissue forming values of expensive and inexpensive foods.*
Use fireless cooker successfully on cereals, meat and vegetables.*
Prepare balanced menu and superintend cooking for one month in home.*
Make delicacies for the sick and send where needed through the National Plant, Flower and Fruit Guild, or through some distributing organization.*
Cook for one month in home.*
Take instructions in a neighbor's home once a week for two months, actually doing the work.*

Marketing: Describe characteristics and identify and select six chief cuts of meat; also state the market price for each.*
Market for one week on one dollar and a half per person, keeping accounts and records of menus, etc.*
Do the same for two dollars.*

Do the same for three dollars.*

Know the best season for the chief fruits and vegetables available in your locality and a reasonable price for each.*

Know the way flour, sugar, rice, cereals, crackers, and breads are sold — packages, bulk, etc.— prices, dangerous and common adulterations.*

Know how to secure full weight and pure food.*

Washing and Ironing: Do a family washing, using modern labor saving devices if possible.*

Wash and iron a shirt waist, a white skirt. Press a skirt and coat.*

Know how to select and use soaps and starches, use stain remover without injury to fabric, know how to wash colored material without loss of color, recognize and know how to soften hard water.*

Housekeeping: Know how to care for hardwood floors, walls, carpets, rugs, hardwood and upholstered furniture.*

Know how to make beds; care of beds for sick, care of baby's bed; airing and changing of bed.*

Know how to sweep and dust, using sweeping compounds, moist cloths, dust absorbing cloths, and principal vacuum cleaners.*

Put away clothing, rugs, furs, blankets, for the summer.*

Know proper disposal of waste and garbage, for home and for city.*

Make a doll's house of four rooms and its furnishings.*

Take instruction in a neighbor's house for one morning a week for two months, actually doing the work.*

Take care of cats or dogs, birds, tame animals, etc., for three months; know what harm they do, what diseases each may carry, and how they may be treated.*

Learn the care of plates, silver, glass, pots, pans, aluminum ware, lamps, copper.*

Invention: Make a useful household invention.*

Entertainment: Play any musical instrument in an orchestra, reading the necessary music.*

Write a poem or words of a song which is either published or adopted for use.*

Commit and recite a thousand lines of standard poetry.*

Have a party of ten with refreshments, costing not more than one dollar; keep accounts.*

Entertain three or more little children for two hours a week for at least two months.*

Know and tell five standard folk stories.*

Write and give a play.*

Plan and give a pantomime entertainment.*

Help in regular visitation and entertainment of the sick in homes, hospitals, or settlements.*

Baby Craft: Know how milk should be prepared for a six months' old baby; know what is good milk for a baby a year old and how it can be tested.*

Know how much a baby should grow in weight each week for the first six months, in height for each month for the first year. The relation of weight to disease and vitality.*

Know and describe three kinds of baby cries and what they mean.*
Care for a baby for an average of an hour a day for a month.*
Make a set of practical playthings for a child three years old.*

NATURE LORE

Trees: Identify and describe any fifteen trees.*
   Plant five trees at least one foot high where they are needed.*

Tramp Lore: Make a satisfactory note book from your own observations while on tramps. This may be on stones, birds, trees, streams, erosion of the earth, or habits of animals.*

Garden: Do all the work in a successful garden. This may be for use or beauty or both.*
   Identify ten common weeds; tell how to remove and eradicate them.*
   Identify ten harmful garden bugs and insects, and tell how to combat them.
   Raise flowers or vegetables in accordance with modern principles, getting cash results — violets, strawberries, celery, mushrooms.*
   Have a successful window garden properly balanced in color or a garden furnishing garnishing for the table. Practical results must be secured.*
   Raise a crop of sweet corn, popcorn, or potatoes. Make a record of processes, history of growth, cost, gain, or loss.*
   Raise at least two vegetables: Make note book record of growth and cost. Can, pickle, and preserve the product to an amount of two quarts canned, two quarts pickled and two quarts preserved.*
   Carry on experimental gardening as follows:
      (a) Plant a plot with seed treated with bacteria solution and another plot with seed not so treated. Record results as to amount of crop, size of product, taste, and palatableness.*
      (b) Plant a plot with pedigreed seeds and another plot with unpedigreed seeds. Record results.*
      (c) Plant two plots. Treat one by dry farming methods, and the other by usual methods. Record results.*
      (d) Make tests of the value of irrigation.*

Stars: Know the planets and seven constellations and their stories.*

Birds: Identify and describe twenty wild birds.*
   Identify and describe fifteen additional wild birds.*
   Erect a bird box and have it used.*
   Tell the value of two birds to man from personal observations and notes.*
   Keep notes from personal observation of the raising of a family of birds.*
   Have a "lunch counter" used by at least four kinds of birds.*

Flowers: Identify and describe twenty wild flowers.*
   Identify and describe fifteen additional wild flowers.*

Bees: Do all the work on a successful hive of bees for a season and know the habits of honey bees.*

Animals: Demonstrate the nature and value of some one factor in heredity or environment in some strain of animals, e. g., chickens, dogs. (Effect of health, breeding, endurance, length of life, color, form or effects of altered food, exercise, out of doors.)*

ELECTIVE HONORS 15

CAMP CRAFT

Tent Craft: Erect and equip a tent, having selected location. Take proper care of tent for one week.*

Wood Craft: Make a shelter and bed of material found in the woods.*

Sleep: Make a bed on the ground and sleep out of doors on it for any five nights.*

Packing: Pack a horse and tie a squaw hitch.*

Fire Lore: Build an open fire in wind and rain with material found out of doors, and build a proper bonfire.* No fire is credited until it is properly left or put out.

Make two good devices for holding a pot over a fire and two for holding a frying pan over a fire.*

Make fire without either fire or matches.

Cooking: Do all the camp cooking without help or advice for one day for four or more persons. This includes getting wood, and making an open fire. Suitable character and variety of foods are to be furnished. The menu must be written; quantities and price stated.*

Weather Lore: Know the meaning of weather signals, and the meaning of clouds, winds, and temperature.*

Keep a scientific weather record for a month. This consists of temperature, wind direction and velocity, clouds, character and quantity, duration of rain fall, fogs or mist.*

Read United States Weather Map for a month and report for each day, comparative record of home point with some distant point.*

Indian Craft: Track two miles.*

Know six Indian legends.*

Know twenty-five signs of the sign language.*

Know six blazes.*

Know three ways the Indians have of testing eyesight.*

Make bead band at least twelve inches long.*

Know fire dance, caribou dance, and eagle dance.*

Make a totem.*

Make an Indian bed.*

Make an Indian tepee.*

Knots: Tie two ends together — square and square bow, single bend or bowline (easily untied), alpine, kite string. Tie a rope to a post or rail or about itself — half hitches (fasten boat or clothesline), clove hitch (fasten horse), midshipman's or rolling hitch (tent rope). Whip a rope to prevent unraveling, with needle and without needle.*

Make knots at the end of a rope — wall knot, crown, back splice. Make two fancy or heraldric knots — carrick bend, love knot (for trimming pillows, shirt waist or dress). Make two trick knots — Tom fools' or sailor's hand cuff, cabin boy's knot. Weave two or more ropes, twine or yarns together — make a plait of three or more strands; make a sennit. Make three kinds of splices; eye, short and long.*

HAND CRAFT

Any article in the following groups must show skill, ingenuity and taste. Each article must be worthy of honor:

Clay Modeling: Model an individual cereal bowl, plate, cup and saucer, having on it original designs, symbolizing some personal characteristic or something about this organization.*

Brass Work: Make a brass or copper bowl or vase having on it original designs.*

Silver Work: Make a set of silver jewelry consisting of bracelet, ring, pin, hat pin, with similar designs.*

Dyeing: Design and dye a headband, a scarf and a pillow cover, preferably using vegetable dyes.*

Stenciling: Stencil a table cover, pillow cover and bureau scarf, with similar designs.*

Basketry: Design and make a basket.*

Wood Carving: Make a useful piece of furniture.*

Carpentry: Make and stain a piece of "Box furniture."*

Toys: Make suitable dolls, picture books and toys and send to hospitals and settlements where they are wanted.*

Sewing: Make two articles of underwear, using hand or machine or both.*
  Make a shirt waist.*
  Make a dress.*
  Make a set of baby clothes.*
  Trim a hat.*
  Save nine stitches once each week for three months.*

Textile Work: Know the prices and widths and uses of the following materials:*

> 12 common cotton materials
> 10 common linen materials
> 6 common woolen materials
> 6 common silk materials

Know how pattern is made in cloth; be able to compare four common textile materials; know their origin, how material is prepared, and how weaving is done.*

BUSINESS

Fill a regular position for four months, earning ten dollars a week or less.**

Fill a regular position for four months, earning more than ten dollars a week.***

Make an article entirely or in part in regular employment, showing skill, speed, and taste. * to * * * * *

Earn three dollars and give it to some worthy cause.*

Earn at least five dollars in any line other than regular employment, e. g., chickens, bees, garden, getting subscribers to books, magazines or papers, making and selling Christmas presents, fancy work, jewelry, toys, dolls.*

Plan expenditure of family under heads of shelter, food, clothing, recreation, miscellaneous.*

Live for one year on an allowance covering all personal expenses. Keep full accounts. * * * * *

Keep a bank account and set aside a definite amount per month for a year.*

PATRIOTISM

Participate in organizing and carrying through, a proper celebration of the
following — in each case the history of the day to be known:
  Independence Day*
  Patriots' Day.*
  Washington's Birthday.*
  Lincoln's Birthday.*
  Labor Day.*
  Memorial Day.*
  Arbor Day.*
  Flag Day.*
Contribute some service to your community in connection with:
  Street Cleaning.*
  Beautifying front yards.*
  Conservation of streams.*
  Conservation of birds.*
  Conservation of trees or forests.*
  Conservation of parks and playgrounds.*
Be familiar with United States history as it affects woman's welfare.*
Know the history of your own locality and what occurred on each historical
  spot.*
Know the history and meaning of the American flag and of the flag of the
  country from which your ancestors came.*
Prepare plans designed to improve the conditions under which girls work in
  your community.*
Commit to memory the Preambles to the Constitution and the Declaration of
  Independence.*

THE COUNCIL FIRE

(Monthly Meeting)

Each Camp Fire shall select or arrange the program and way of carrying on its own meetings. It will add much to the interest to have each Camp Fire have some original ceremonies. The meetings may be conducted in the usual way with a chairman, secretary, etc., or some more picturesque form may be chosen. The following ceremonial form is not required, it is intended to be suggestive:

1. The Preparation of the Fire:

>   The wood and kindling are brought to the hearth by the Wood Gatherers. (Where a fire is not possible candles may be used. Even one candle may sym—bolize the Fire.)

>   The Fire Makers arrange the wood for lighting or place the candles in order.

>   The Fire is lighted by a Torch Bearer appointed by the Guardian or by the Guardian herself.

2. The Gathering of the Girls:

>   When the hour has arrived and all is ready, the Guardian calls the girls to gather around the place of the Fire This call may be a song, a chant, or a call on some musical instrument.

3. The Lighting of the Fire

> When all are seated around the place of the fire, a Torch Bearer or the Guardian lights the fire. This may be done with matches, but better still it may be started with the rubbing of sticks. If directions are carefully followed it is not difficult to learn this method of starting a fire. After the fire is lighted the ceremony is completed by the group repeating the following ode in unision.

[When candles are used in place of the fire the Wohelo ceremony may be adopted. See page 20.]

ODE TO FIRE

Oh Fire !

> Long years ago when our fathers fought with great animals you were their great protection.
>
> When they fought the cold of the cruel winter you saved them.
>
> When they needed food you changed the flesh of beasts into savory meat for them.
>
> During all the ages your mysterious flame has been a symbol to them for Spirit.
>
> So (to-night) we light our fire in grateful remembrance of the Great Spirit who gave you to us.

4. Roll Call:

> In some camps each girl may win a new name when she becomes a Fire Girl. This name is used only among the Fire Girls. Names from any language may be used. Descriptive names may be won and awarded for some achievement. Indian names may be given,

such as Wap-o, Sunbeam; Wap-O-Mi-O, Happy
Bird; Wa-wa, duck; Sun Sister; Star Sister; Song
Flower; Shining Eyes.

Camp Fire Count or Official Roll:

Each Camp Fire shall have an official roll in which
shall be recorded all the official doings; election
and initiation of members, new names if any are given
special attainments of individuals, the names of those
who have been given honors, and the individual honors
and ranks awarded. If there is an artistic girl in
the group the book may become one of the most
treasured possessions, for in it can be illustrations of
various doings and attainments. It may be written
in poetic form. There may be photographs and
decorations, and a cover on which the symbol peculiar
to that particular Camp Fire may be worked out in
conventional form.

5. Reports of the Girls:

Report of the last Council Fire and of the weekly
meetings. This is written by the girls in rotation
Sometimes it is written in rhyme or verse. Each girl
is to tell of some kind deed which she has seen done
since the last meeting. She should also state in what
way if any she indicated her appreciation of the act
New or unfinished business; suggestions.

6. Awarding of Honors. Initiation of new members, be—
stowal of new names.

7. The Fire Story or Talk.

8. Ceremony, Songs, and Toasts.

9. At the close of each talk on any part of the Law, each
   girl shall stand, place her right hand over heart and
   repeat the following:

> This Law of the Fire
> I will strive to follow
> With all the strength
> And endurance of my body,
> The power of my will,
> The keenness of my mind,
> The warmth of my heart,
> And the sincerity of my spirit.

10. The Fire is extinguished and the hearth left in order.

THE WOHELO CEREMONY

The Wohelo ceremony is intended to show how a picturesque
form may be given to a very simple act — the lighting of the
candles. It is desirable to have each meeting open with some
little ceremony, for beauty and dignity are gained thereby.
This particular ceremony can be used only when the meeting is
around the candles. [It takes the place of section three, The
Lighting of the Fire in the Council Fire.]

Place three candles in the centre of the circle. One stands for
Work, one for Health and one for Love. A taper is lighted by
the Guardian and is handed to one of the girls, who steps to the
centre of the circle, kneels on one knee, and says:

"I light the light of Work, for Wohelo
means work."

She lights one candle.   She then says:

> "Wohelo means work.
>> We glorify work because through
>> work we are free.   We work to
>> win, to conquer, to be masters.
>> We work for the joy of the work-
>> ing and because we are free.
>
> "Wohelo means work."

She then retires and her place is taken by a second girl, whc comes forward and says:

> "I light the light of Health, for Wohelo
means health."

After lighting the candle she says:

> "Wohelo means health.
>> We hold on to health, because
>> through health we serve and are
>> happy.   In caring for the health
>> and beauty of our persons we are
>> caring for the very shrine of the
>> Great Spirit.
>
> "Wohelo means health."

Then she retires.   A third girl comes forward and says:

> "I light the light of Love, for Wohelo
means love."

After lighting the last candle she says:

"Wohelo means love.

> We love Love, for love is life,
> and light and joy and sweetness.
> And love is comradeship and motherhood,
> and fatherhood and all dear kinship.
> Love is the joy of service so deep
> that self is forgotten.

"Wohelo means love."

After the lighting of the candles the Wohelo musical cheer is given.

WOHELO FOR AYE!

Music from Aloha.

The musical cheer is sung twice, the first line in unison and the second line in parts. Ordinarily the words, "Wohelo for aye," are used throughout. For ceremonial occasions the words, "Wohelo for work, Wohelo for health, Wohelo for love," are used the second time the cheer is sung as written above.

COUNCIL FIRE TALKS

Talks may be given about the Council Fire by the Guardian, by a visitor or sometimes by a girl, or there may be a general discussion. The general idea of the talks should be to enlarge ideals and to inspire effort. The following are offered as suggestions for such talks.

Suggestions for Talks About the Law

Seek Beauty.— Demand beauty in all of life. Where it is lacking help create it; where it is present appreciate it. We must embody it in our actions; we must see it in nature and in people, and we must love it in our hearts.

We must learn to see the beauty in our surroundings; in the beautiful proportions of trees and buildings; in the colors of sky and water; in shadow and light, storm and sunshine. We should seek beauty in dress. The way a girl dresses and walks proclaims to any one who sees her deep facts about her inmost self. Dignity, beauty, and modesty express themselves in good taste in dress. We must learn that the deepest beauty is within and that what we see outside is after all only a reflection of ourselves.

Give Service.— Service is meaningless unless it grows out of or grows into love of others. A mother who takes care of her

24

child because it is her duty is missing what is most vital: to realize the wonder of a little child, and to know that the greatest service one can render God and man is to watch the unfolding of a soul and with kind understanding help it to grasp the right meaning of life.

"Love your neighbor," and service will be as unconscious and beautiful as the service of a father or mother, brother, sister or friend. Therefore let us seek to establish love in our hearts; service will follow. Though not so easy, the opposite is true: serve your neighbor and love will follow.

Pursue Knowledge.— Much that we learn seems to have no bearing on life. At best, we cannot acquire all knowledge; but at this time, when the world is readjusting itself so rapidly and extensively to woman and her work, women need the guidance of expert knowledge that they may apply themselves to life as effectively as possible. The Law tells us to learn those things which are most important for us to know, in order that we may be able, useful and efficient in the world.

Be Trustworthy.— Be in truth what you wish to seem. Hate all sham and pretense. Be-worthy-of-trust. This Law teaches us not to undertake enterprises rashly, but having undertaken something, to complete it unflinchingly. This will teach us to be loyal to other women, to our own highest ideals, and to all which commands our approval. We bring honor and credit to the Camp Fire Girls by being worthy-to-be-trusted.

Hold on to Health.— It is difficult under present conditions to keep ourselves thoroughly well. The Law lays great emphasis on this: that we may dress wisely, that we shall be guided rightly in our eating and sleeping, in our exercise, in the intimate care of our bodies, and in self-knowledge.

The woman with fine health has advantages in almost every way. The lives of many women are marked by the tombstones of splendid things which they attempted to do but in which they failed because of ill health.

Glorify Work.— To many people work is mere drudgery. We think of the necessity of work as a curse laid on man; whereas work is really one of the most splendid gifts to man. Without adequate work life is meaningless, restless, without satisfaction or achievement. Work is to be dignified and glorified and done so splendidly that it shall be lifted from the plane of necessity to that of opportunity.

Be Happy.— The Law teaches us to be happy; if we have pain, to hide it; if others have sorrow, to be quick to relieve it. It teaches us to smile because life is full of joy: that joy which is based on health, work, and love.

QUESTIONS AND ANSWERS

ORGANIZATION

What is the first step?

Application should be made to the Adviser, if there is one in the community, or to the National Headquarters. In general it is advisable to organize in connection with some existing organization, such as a school or the Young Women's Christian Association.

Can mothers organize a group of girls in their community?

Several mothers may organize a group of girls, planning the meetings, to be held in the different homes, and conferring together as to the activities. One of the mothers should qualify as Guardian in the usual way. Each mother in turn may train the girls in those branches in which she is proficient.

How can members of a playground, a Young Women's Christian Association, a school, a church, a Sunday School or a Social Centre organize?

By securing the approval and co-operation of the head of the institution, who will take the responsibility and secure information from National Headquarters. It is possible in any of these institutions to have as many Camp Fires as desirable.

Let us take a single illustration: Public Schools in a given city may wish to have a number of Camp Fire groups.

One woman should be responsible for the general management of all these groups of girls. She shall be appointed as Chief Guardian by the Adviser for the city upon the nomination of the superintendent of schools or some person in like authority. Under her supervision the various Camp Fires will be conducted by their respective Guardians so that there will be a Public School group of Camps. Any other kind of association may organize similarly.

How can an independent group of girls organize?

They should communicate with the Adviser if there is one in their community or, if not, write directly to the National Headquarters for instructions.

What is the plan of organization for a whole city?

In cities of considerable size there may be an Adviser who is appointed by the national body.

In some cities it may be desirable to have an Advisory Board. A Committee on Organization composed of from three to ten interested men and women shall nominate for membership on the Advisory Board from six to fifty representative men and women. In some cases the Advisory Board might have as many as a hundred members. The nominations shall be sent to the national body, by whom the official appointments are made. The Committee on Organization is dissolved after the Advisory Board has been appointed. From the Advisory Board a Chief Adviser is nominated for appointment by the national body. Some of the sources from which to select members for such Advisory Boards are:

Churches

Young Women's Catholic Associations

Young Women's Christian Associations

Young Women's Hebrew Associations
Schools
Settlements
Village Improvement Societies
Playground Associations
Colleges
Charity Organizations
Granges
Town Historical Societies
Daughters of the American Revolution
Woman's Clubs
Women's Christian Temperance Unions
District Nurses' Associations, etc.
Epworth League
Christian Endeavor

The Advisory Board, or the Adviser where there is no Board, shall have charge of the organization of all Camp Fires in the city.

What are the duties of the Chief Adviser?

The Chief Adviser presides at the meetings of the Advisory Board; signs Guardians' applications to be sent to National Headquarters; confers with the Guardians; and gives advice to those desiring to qualify for leadership.

What are the duties of the Advisory Board?

It meets at least once a month; supervises the local Camp Fires; chooses and recommends the Guardian of the Fires, makes a survey of the community with reference to forming new Fires; provides financial help when needed, creates public interest in the Camp Fire Girls.

What is the ranking order?

Immediately in contact with the girls themselves is the Guardian. A group of Guardians in some one organization will have a Chief Guardian, and over the work in an entire city will be the Adviser or Advisory Board.

How much organization is necessary?

Not all of these sub-divisions will be needed in every community. Small communities will need nothing but a Guardian, and for most communities an Adviser to look after the general interests and the Guardian to look after the girls will be all that is necessary.

CHIEF GUARDIANS

What are the duties of a Chief Guardian?

She is responsible for a group of Camps within ·some one general organization — i. e., a school, playground association, etc. She is appointed from the National Headquarters upon nomination by the head of the organization or some like authority.

GUARDIANS

What are the qualifications of a Guardian of the Fire?

The first qualification is that she shall know and love the girls. It is important that she have the out-of-door spirit and be somewhat familiar with the out-of-door life and activities; and that she understand the meaning of the home and the opportunities for doing important things in the home in an interesting way. She should be a woman who wants to be with girls because she enjoys it, rather than merely because she thinks it her duty. The greater her enthusiasm and health, the better — the more natural her leadership, the better.

This organization cannot be held together by bonds of duty. Both girls and Guardians must find in it that which is so splendidly attractive that they will enjoy spending a reasonable amount of time in this way.

How may a Guardian be appointed?

To become a Guardian one must receive appointment from the National Headquarters, this appointment to hold good for one year. The Guardian's application must have the endorsement of the Adviser, or the Advisory Board if there is one. National authorization in any case is necessary, for some may wish to lead Camp Fire groups who are not suited in character or ability for this responsible work. The character, power and enthusiasm of the Guardians of the Fire are more important than anything else in the whole organization. Unless the Guardians are enthusiastic, intelligent and devoted to the best things it is better not to have the organization at all. All the rest of the machinery is for the purpose of bringing the right kind of women, as Guardians, into contact with the girls themselves.

Can the girls elect their own Guardians?

They may ask for the appointment of some one whom they desire, and the probability is that such person will receive appointment, but the girls themselves cannot elect their superior officers.

What are the duties of the Guardian of the Fire?

The Guardian meets the girls weekly at least; sees that proper preparations are made for the meeting; selects those who shall perform the different duties; plans the work; sees that the practice for the attainment of honors is properly carried on; conducts the exercises for the initiation of new members;

and in general is responsible for all the activities of a Camp Fire. This does not mean that she herself must know and do all the various things that are put down under the Elective Honors. No one person can know or do all of these things, but a Guardian should be able to do some of them herself and to find other women in the community who will help with special ones. For example, if the girls want to learn folk dancing and the Guardian herself is not able to teach them, she may be able to find some one who can do this. She should know how to find and refer to books and magazines containing helpful articles on the activities to be taken up. When possible she should take the girls on tramps or out-of-door expeditions.

To whom are the Guardians of the Fire responsible?

The Guardians of the Fire are ultimately responsible to the national body, but in cities where there are Advisers or an Advisory Board they are directly responsible to them.

May one Guardian lead more than one Camp Fire?

A Guardian may be able to direct more than one Camp Fire, but in general she should not have more than three. Each group should have at least one meeting a week. Occasionally she may wish to have them all together for some general expedition, or other co-operative work.

MEMBERSHIP QUALIFICATIONS

How old must a girl be to join a Camp Fire?

There is no definite age limit. Some of the activities are suitable for younger girls and some for older ones. In general the activities are adapted to girls who are in their teens.

ACTIVITIES AND HONORS

Do the girls in a given Camp Fire have to do the same things?

No. What they do will depend upon the available facilities that they have and upon the skill of the Guardian.

In order to win certain of these honors technical knowledge is required; in order to win others, particular capacity. The field is restricted in no way except by natural limitations.

For example, girls who live where there is no water can hardly be expected to get honors in water sports.

Are the Camps self-governing?

They are in all minor matters. That is, the Guardian must, in most respects, use her best judgment as to what and how much the girls shall do, but in the general plan the rules of the entire organization shall be followed. No Guardian has a right to set aside the conditions of membership or the specified requirements for attaining the different ranks, or any other matter of a general character.

Who decides whether or not a girl has won an honor which she claims?

This is to be decided by the Guardian. She may call in any assistance which she wishes, but the responsibility rests on her to see that high standards are maintained.

How are honors awarded?

When a Guardian of the Fire is satisfied that a given honor has been adequately won, she will tell the candidate to step forward at the next Council Fire, when she will tell all the girls of that Camp Fire that ———— has won a given honor in such and such a craft. For each group of the seven elective honors there is a special colored bead.

Health — Bright red

Homecraft — Orange

Nature lore — Sky blue

Campcraft — Wood brown

Handcraft — Green

Business — Black and gold

Patriotism — Red, white and blue

This means that each girl may win seven chains of beads. For example, in Homecraft it is possible to win a necklace of fifty beads.

How are the different ranks designated?

When a girl becomes a Wood Gatherer she is entitled to wear a wood brown emblem representing the crossed wood on her left arm. This is the official emblem of the Wood Gatherer's rank. She is also entitled to wear a silver ring on which is a bunch of fagots. Both of these can be secured from Headquarters. While the ring is official, it is not required.

When a girl becomes a Fire Maker she is entitled to add to the Wood Gatherer's emblem the blue, green and touch of orange which represents the flame. She is also entitled to wear the Fire Maker's bracelet, but this is not required.

When a girl becomes a Torch Bearer she is entitled to wear the full insignia, which consists of a touch of white, representing the smoke from the flame, added to the Fire Maker's emblem. She is also entitled to wear the silver pin of the Torch Bearer. This is not required.

GENERAL

Where are the meetings held?

They are held in any available place, indoors or out. Many of these meetings will be in homes, others in summer camps.

They are held in the suburbs when girls go out for holiday tramps. They are held in school buildings.

Should there not be a fee which each girl must pay?

Each group is entirely free in this respect. If a given group of girls want to require a fee, devoting this money to some common good, or to some special piece of work in the community, there is no reason why they should not do so, but it is not required by the national organization. Whatever money is contributed by the girls themselves should be spent as they themselves may determine.

Is there an official uniform as there is for the Boy Scouts?

There is an official outdoor suit, an official swimming suit, and an official ceremonial dress. None of these is required. The wearing of the uniform is optional with the group or the individual girl. They are desirable because wearing them creates a certain *esprit de corps*. Better clothing is secured in this way than can be secured elsewhere for the same money. The cermonial dress is made by the girls themselves from patterns furnished by the national organization.

Canticle of the Sun

O most high, almighty good Lord God, to Thee belong praise, glory, honor, and all blessing!

Praised be my Lord God with all His creatures, especially our brother the Sun who brings us the day and who brings us the Light; fair is he and shines with a very great splendor; O Lord, he signifies to us Thee!

Praised be my Lord for our sister the moon, and for the stars, the which He has set clear and lovely in heaven.

Praised be my Lord for our brother the wind, and for air, and cloud, calms and all weather by which Thou upholdest life in all creatures.

Praised be my Lord for our sister the water, who is very serviceable unto us and humble and precious and clean.

Praised be my Lord for our brother fire, through whom Thou givest us Light in the darkness; and he is bright and pleasant and very mighty and strong.

Praised be my Lord for our mother the earth, the which doth sustain us and keep us, and bringeth forth divers fruits and flowers of many colors, and grass.

Praised be my Lord for all those who pardon one another for His love's sake, and who endure weakness and tribulation; blessed are they who peaceably shall endure, for Thou, O most Highest, shalt give them a crown.

Praise ye and bless the Lord, and give thanks unto Him and serve Him with great humility

— *St. Francis of Assisi.*

Lay me to sleep in sheltering flame,
  O Master of the Hidden Fire;
Wash pure my heart, and cleanse for me
  My soul's desire.

In flame of sunrise bathe my mind,
  O Master of the Hidden Fire,
That, when I wake, clear-eyed may be
  My soul's desire.

                              —Fiona Macleod.

BOOKS FOR REFERENCE

The following is a brief suggested bibliography covering some of the main points brought out in the list of " activities."

HEALTH CRAFT

American Red Cross...Red Cross Text Book for
First Aid...............American   Red
Cross......... $0.30
Blaikie ....How to Get Strong and How
to Stay So ....Harper & Bros... 1.00
Blaikie. ....Sound Bodies for Boys and
Girls. ....American   Book
Co...........   .40
Carpenter, Frank, G. ..Foods and Their Uses .....Chas. Scribner's
Sons.........   .50
"   "   " ..How the World is Fed......American Book
Co...........   .60
Corsan, G. H.........'.At Home in the Water......Y. M. C. A. Press   .50
Dalton. ....How to Swim.............G. P. Putnam's
Sons........ 1.00
Fisher, Herbert W. ...Making Life Worth While...Doubleday, Page
& Co.......... 1.20
Galbraith, Anna.......Personal Hygiene and
Physical Training for
Women................W.B. Saunders Co. 2.00
Gulick, C. V..........Emergencies...............Ginn & Co. 40
Gulick, L. H., M. D....The Efficient Life. ....Doubleday, Page
& Co........ 1.20
Jewett, Mrs. Frances...The Body and Its Defences Ginn & Co.   .65
"   "   "   The Body at Work........   "   "   .50
"   "   "   Good Health.............   "   "   .40
"   "   "   Town and City...........   "   "   .40
Sargent, Dudley.......Health, Strength, and
Power..................H. M.Caldwell Co. 1.50

GAMES AND FOLK DANCING

Bancroft, Jessie H. ....Games and Plays for Home..Macmillan Co... 1.50
Burchenal, Elizabeth ..Folk-Dances and Singing
Games...............G. Schirmer..... 1.50
Crampton, C. Ward ...Folk Dance Book..........A. S. Barnes Co. 1.50

Crawford, Caroline ...Folk Dances and Games.....A. S. Barnes Co. 1.50
Gulick, L. H. ....Healthful Art of Dancing...Doubleday, Page
                                   & Co....... 1.25
Hofer, Marie.........Children's Singing Games. ..Hofer.......... .50
Johnson, G. E.. ....Education by Plays and
                     Games.................Ginn & Co. ..... .90

HOME CRAFT

Beard Lina and Adelia..Handicraft and Recreation for
                     Girls..................Chas. Scribner's
                               Sons.......... 1.60
                     A book of general suggestions as to how to do a
                     variety of things with simple materials.
Busbey Katherine, G ..Home Life in America. .....Macmillan Co... 2.00
                     A general bird's eye view of American home con-
                     ditions written in an entertaining fashion.
                     Good for general reference.
Burrell, C. B.........Saturday Mornings.........Dana Estes Co.. .75
                     A capital book telling how a young girl was
                     trained to do household things in a series of de-
                     lightful Saturday mornings with her mother.
Campbell, Helen ......American Girl's Home .....G. P. Putnam's
                               Sons.......... 1.75
                     Book of Work and Play. A miscellaneous col-
                     lection suggestive of "things to do" by way of
                     simple occupation and amusement.
Earl, Alice Morse......Home Life in Colonial Days.Macmillan Co.. 2.50
                     Gives a delightful account of home making in the
                     olden days, with beautiful illustrations of old-
                     time furniture and home industries, and word
                     pictures of such old-fashioned industries as
                     candle-making, hand-weaving, and spinning.
Farmer, Fannie Merritt. The Boston Cooking School Little, Brown &
                     Cook Book. .... Co........... 2.00
Foster, Olive H.......Cookery for Little Girls.....Duffield & Co.... .75
Haskins, C. W........How to Keep Household
                     Accounts...............Harper & Bros... 1.00
                     A simple practical exposition.
Johnston, Constance. ..When Mother Lets Us Help. Moffatt, Yard &
                             Co.......... .75
Kirkland, E. S........Six Little Cooks ....A. C. McClurg
                     A story.   & Co......... .75
L. Ray Balderston
M. C. Limerick ....Laundry Manual.....John C. Winston
                             Co, Phila.... .60
Lloyd, Mrs. E. B. ...."Grandma's Cook Book,"................. 1.25
                     A hand volume containing many receipts.
Meldrum, D. S........Home Life in Holland.......Macmillan Co.... 1.75
                     Gives a delightful intimate portrayal of Holland
                     home life.

Rankin, C. W..........Dandelion Cottage..........Henry Holt & Co.   1.50
    An excellent story of the way in which four girls
    played at housekeeping.

Springsted, Anna F ...The Expert Waitress. .... Harper & Bros.   100
    Simple rules for correct service given in a direct
    way.

Wiggin, K. D.........Half a Dozen Housekeepers..A. C. McClurg &
    Co. 75
    A jolly story of the haps and mishaps of six girls
    who experiment at housekeeping.

The American School of Home Economics in Chicago issues a very desirable set of books touching on different phases of home life. They are here listed under *Home Craft* as a series:

(a) The House: Its plan, decoration and care. Isabel Bevier........   1.50
    A short history of the evolution of the House and the development of the American Home. It contains plans for simple homes, suggestions as to home decorations, furniture.

(b) Household Hygiene. S. Maria Elliot........................   1.25

(c) Home Care of the Sick. Amy E. Pope.......................   1.00
    A practical little treatise of "How to Do It" in simple cases of home nursing.

(d) Household Bacteriology. S. M. Elliot. 1.50
    Shows the relation between hygiene and bacteriology and the daily task of housekeeping. Treats of dust heaps, preserving of foods, milk.

(e) Personal Hygiene. Maurice Le Bosquet, T. B...............   1.50
    A compact little treatise on health and how to keep it...

(f) Food and Dietetics. Alice Peloubet Horton, M. D...........
    Takes up such problems of food and dietetics as, cost of food, principles of food, relation of food to the body, dietary standards.

(g) Chemistry of Household. Margaret E. Dodd, A. B...........   1.50
    Treats of the chemistry of water, food, lighting, in relation to the household; and also of such practical things as cleansing, stains, etc.

(h) Textiles and Clothing. K. H. Watson......................   1.95
    Gives primitive methods, and treats of modern process in weaving, sewing.

(i) Household Management. Bertha M. Terrill.................   1.50
    Takes up in a simple and practical way such problems as household management, expenditure, rent, accounts, marketing and food economy.

NATURE LORE

Adams...............Harpers' Outdoor Book for
    Boys...................Harper & Bros... 1.75
    Contains many good suggestions concerning camp life which may easily be adapted for girls in camp life.

Lounsbury, Alice.......A Guide to Trees..........F. A. Stokes Co.. 1.75
Lounsbury, Alice.......The Garden Book for Young
                        People................F. A. Stokes Co.. 1.50
                        (In story form.)
Martin...............The Friendly Stars.........Harper & Bros... 1.25
Mathews, F. S.........Familiar Trees and Their
                        Leaves.................D. Appleton & Co 1.75
Mathews, F. S.........Field Book of American
                        Wildflowers.............G. P. Putnam's
                                                    Sons.......... 1.75
Newcomb, G..........Popular Astronomy........Harper & Bros.... 2.50
Reed, Chester A.......Flower Guide............Chester A. Reed,
                                                    Worcester
Reed, Chester A.......Bird Guide.............Chester A. Reed
                                                    Worcester...   .50
                        Part 1. Water Birds.....
                         "   2. Land Birds......   .50
Roberts, C. D.........Heart of the Ancient Wood..Grosset & Dunlap .50
                        This is a beautiful story of life in the deep woods,
                        containing much valuable information on the
                        subject of the "shy wild things" and a little
                        girl's intimate knowledge of them.
Rogers, Julia E.......The Tree Book............Doubleday, Page
                                                    & Co. 4.00
Porter, Gene Stratton..Freckles ....   "   "   1.20
Porter, Gene Stratton. Girl of the Limberlost....... "   "   1.20
                        An excellent story of a girl's love of nature and
                        what she found through that love. A story of
                        the woods and of the insect and four-footed
                        creation
Seton, Ernest Thomp-
  son................Sign Language ....Doubleday, Page
                                                    & Co.
Seton, Ernest Thomp- International Code of
  son .... Signals. ....Gov't Printing
                                                    Office, Wash-
                                                    ington, D. C...
Seton, Ernest Thomp- Life Histories of Northern
  son .... Animals 18.00
White, Stewart
  Edward ....The Mountains ....Doubleday, Page
                                                    & Co........ 1.50
White, Stewart
  Edward ....The Blazed Trail.........Doubleday, Page
                                                    & Co. 1.50
                        His intimate acquaintance with the woodways,
                        his vivid power of description and his sym-
                        pathetic insight into the wood life make his
                        works of value.
Wright, M. C. ....Fourfooted Americans.......Macmillan Co... 1.50

Wright, Mabel Osgood..Tommy Anne and the Three
Hearts.................Macmillan Co... 1.50
A good story concerning a little girl whose love
and interest opened the way into the Heart o'
Nature, Heart o' Man and Heart o' God, and
found the relation between them.

HAND CRAFT

Buins, C. F.   ....The Potter's Craft.........D. Van Nostrand
Co............ .50
Christie, A. N..........Embroidery and Tapestry
Weaving...............Macmillan Co.... 2.00
Davidson.............Concrete Pottery and
Garden Furniture. ....Munns & Co. ...
Featherston, F. C......Guide to Pyrography for
Students and Amateurs...E. Weber & Co... .60
A good manual for the art of   Artists' Material
wood burning.   and Draughts-
man's Supplies,
1125 Chesnut
Street, Phila-
delphia.
Firth, Annie..........Cane Basket Work 1st & 2nd
Series...................Chas.   Scribner's
Sons......... .60
An excellent book suggesting many variations
of this delightful and easy kind of basketry.
Hooper, Luther ....Hand-Loom Weaving.......Macmillan Co... 2.25
A compact description of weaving.
James, George Wharton How to Make Indian Baskets Henry Malkan... 1.00
Jenks, Tudor..........Photography for Young
People.................F. A. Stokes Co. 1.50
Kelley, L. E...........A Hundred Things a Bright
Girl Can Do............Dana Estes Co... 1.00
Kilbon...............Elementary Woodwork......Lothrop, Lee &
Shepard Co.... .75
Leland, Godfrey, Chas..Wood Carving for Young
People.................Photo.—Beacon Co. .45
Tribune Building. Chicago,
25c. a copy, $10 a year.
McCormick, M.. ......Spool Knitting.. ....A. S. Barnes Co.. 1.00
A good book on the old-fashioned child-art of
spool knitting.
McGlauflin, Isabelle ..Handicraft for Girls. ....Manual Arts.... 1.00
Press, Peoria, Ill.
A tentative course in needlework, basketry,
designing, paper and card board construction,
textiles, fibres, and fabrics, and home decora-
tion.   An excellent guide book for general use.

Morgan, M. H........How to Dress a Doll........Henry Altemus Co .50
        A good book for guiding a child's experimental
        efforts in making doll clothes, leading up to
        simple ways of dressmaking.

Noyes, Wm...........Hand Work in Wood........Manual Art Press. 2.00

Noyes, Wm...........Woodwork for Beginners....

Taylor ....Why My Photographs are
                 Bad. ....Jacobs & Co.Phila 1.00

Wheeler, Candace ....How to Make Rugs........Doubleday, Page
                           & Co. 1.00
        A simple hand book on the popular art of
        rug making.

CAMP CRAFT

Gibson, H. W. ....Camp Life in the Woods....Boy Scout Manual
                         Ch. 11........ .25

Kephart, Horace .....The Book of Camping and
               Woodcraft...............Camping Outing
                         Co. 2.00

Kephart, Horace .....Camp Cookery ....Outing Co....... 1.50
        A practical treatise for camp life.

Price, Overton W......The Land We Live In.......Small, Maynard
                         Co............ 1.50
        A boy's book on conservation, but fully as useful
        in a girl's club. An excellent treatment of the
        subject.

Roth, Filbert ....First Book of Forestry......Ginn & Co. ..... .75
        An excellent general survey of our American
        forestry as to beauty and utility.

Seton, Ernest Thomp-
  son ....Woodcraft ....Boy Scout Manual
                         Ch. 11 .... .25

     "   "   Ropes, Knotting and
        Splicing, etc.............Boy Scout Manual .25

BIOGRAPHY

Audubon, Lucy ....John James Audubon.......G. P. Putnam's
                         Sons.......... 1.50

Brooks, E. S. ....Historic Girls.............G. P. Putnam's
                         Sons......... 1.25

Cheney, Laura........Louisa Alcott, Her Life and
               Letters ....Little, Brown &
                         Co............ 1.50

Keller, Helen ....Story of My Life...........Doubleday, Page
                         & Co. 1.50

Larcom, Lucy.........A New England Girlhood....Houghton, Mifflin
                         Co........... .75

Lang, Andrew.........Life of Jeanne d'Arc. 3.50
Mabie, Hamilton. .....Heroines Every Child
                      Should Know...........Doubleday, Page
                                             & Co. .... .90
Palmer, Alice ....The Life of Alice Freeman
                      Palmer ....Houghton, Mifflin
                                             Co........... 1.50
Perry, Frances and
  Beebe, Katherine....Four Great American Presi-
                      dents.................American Book
                                             Co........... .50
Richards, Laura E. ....Florence Nightingale........D. Appleton & Co 1.25
Tappan, Eva May.....In the Days of Queen
                      Victoria...............Lothrop, Lee &
                                             Shepard Co... .80

FICTION FOR YOUNGER GIRLS

Catherwood, M. H.....Rocky Fork...............Lothrop, Lee &
                                             Shepard Co. .. 1.50
Collodi.............Pinocchio: The Adventures
                      of a Marionette.........Ginn & Co. 1.00
Craik, D. M..........Little Lame Prince........Harper & Bros... .60
De la Ramé, L. ....Bimbi Stories.............Ginn & Co. ..... .50
Dix, B. H............Merry Lips...............Macmillan Co... 1.50
Kirkland, Winifred ...Home Comers.............Houghton, Mifflin
                                             Co........ 1.20
Lorenzini, Carlo.......Adventures of Pinocchio....Doubleday, Page
                                             & Co........ .90
Mac Donald, Geo......At the Back of the North
                      Wind..................Routledge....... .75
Shaw, F. L..........Castle Blair..............Little, Brown &
                                             Co......... 1.00
Spyri, Joanna. ....Heidi....................Ginn & Co. ..... .75
Tappan, Eva May......Robin Hood, His Book ...Little, Brown &
                                             Co........... 1 50

OLD-FASHIONED TALES

Ewing, Mrs...........Jan of the Windmill.......Little, Brown &
                                             Co......... .50
Lucas, E. V..........Forgotten Tales of Long Ago. Hokes........... 1.50
Molesworth, M. L. ....Carrotts..................T. Y. Crowell Co. .75
Sherwood, Mrs........The Fairchild Family.......Hokes........... 1.50

DRAMATICS

Chubb, Percival.......Festival Life Series.........Ethical Culture
                                             School.......
Dalkeith ....Little Plays. ....E. P. Dutton & Co .50
Lena................Historic Incidents ....
                      Excellent guide.

MacKay, Constance D..House of the Heart.........Henry Holt & Co. 1.10
                     A classic. Adapted to girls. Type of old
                     morality plays.
Stevenson, Augusta....Children's Classics in
                     Dramatic Form............Houghton, Mif-
                     flin Co. Excellent for bringing out heroic
                     elements in womanhood.
                         Vol. 1.............................. .35
                          "   2.............................. .35
                          "   3.............................. .50

READ-OUT-LOUD BOOKS FOR AROUND THE CAMP FIRE

Abbott, Eleanor Hallo-
    well..... ....Molly Make-Believe.......Century Co..... 1.00
Blackmore, R. D.......Lorna Doone. ....Chas. Scribner's
                                               Sons.......... 1.00
Chapin, A. A.........Story of the Rhinegold .....Harper & Bros... 1.25
Craik, D. M..........John Halifax Gentlemen.....Dodd,Mead & Co. .75
Dickens, Charles .....Little Dorrit ....Harper & Bros... 1.00
Eliot, George........Romola...................Harper & Bros... .75
Fuller, Z. A..........A Venetian June..........G. P. Putnam's
                                               Sons.......... 1.25
Fox, John Jr.........Little Shepherd of Kingdom
                     Come..................Chas. Scribner's
                                               Sons 1.50
Hale, Lucretia ....Peterkin Papers...........Houghton Mifflin
                                               Co........... 1.50
Howard, Blanche Willis.One Summer ....Houghton Mifflin
                                               Co........... 1.00
Howard, Blanche Willis.The Open Door...........Houghton Mifflin
                                               Co........... 1.50
Marlitt........... ...Old Mamselle's Secret.......A. L. Burt & Co. .75
Marlitt..............Little Moorland Princess....A. L. Burt & Co. .75
Montgomery..........Anne of Green Gables......Page 1.50
Reed, Myrtle ....The Master's Violin. ....G. P. Putnam's
                                               Sons.......... 1.50
Little, Frances........The Lady of the Decoration..Century Co..... 1.00

GENERAL

Addams, Jane.........The Spirit of Youth in the
                     City Streets. ....Macmillan Co... 1.25
Addams, Jane.........Twenty Years in Hull House.Macmillan Co... 2.50
Betts, Lillian W.......The Leaven in a Great City. Dodd,Mead & Co. 1.50
                     Gives sympathetic glimpses of the lower life in
                     New York and shows the different agencies at
                     work for social betterment.

Brush, C. C. ....The Colonel's Opera Cloak ...Little, Brown &
                                  Co............ 1.00
Loane, M.............The Queen's Poor..........Longmans Green
                                  & Co......... 1.25
                     A sympathetic portrayal of the life of the poor
                     in London.
Mangold ....Child Problems.............Macmillan Co... 1.25
                     Gives a general view of problems connected with
                     child welfare in a great city.

INDEX OF SUBJECTS

Photographs of Camp Fire Girls

THE HAND SIGN OF CAMP FIRE
In the first position the fingers of the right hand are flattened
against the fingers of the left, indicating the crossed wood

In the second position the hand is raised following the curves
of an imaginary flame

A Camp Fire Girl in ceremonial dress and head band

Made by a true Camp Fire Girl

A Camp Fire Girl enjoying nature

Fire maiden with rubbing sticks for making fire

This girl has tipped over her canoe and has righted it and is now splashing the water out. If she splashes enough water from the canoe to enable her to sit on the seat and paddle to shore she will receive an honor

Doll house. Furniture made with a scroll saw from cigar boxes

Furniture of a doll's bedroom. Motif: "Baby's Boat's
a Silver Moon"

These girls have slept out on the top of a mountain and are now on their way down

Brushing teeth before a morning dip

A shelter built by the girls

All girls enjoy wading

A bacon bat

Bacon on a stick ready to broil

A leisure hour

It is always a happy "good morning" after a night
sleeping out

A corn roast

One method of roasting corn

A tent with the sides rolled up

Wash day. Each girl does her own

Columbus Day

Drinking from a leaf cup

Ready for a night in the open

First aid to the injured

Making symbolic bead bands on bead looms

Paddling in the war canoe

Preparing an Independence Day fire

A hay-rack ride

Making blue prints of ferns and leaves of trees

Winning honors at the typewriter

Playing games in a meadow

Children's pets

A tomato club

Serving a picnic lunch

A gipsy trip

Mending a canoe

Planting a tree

Folk dancing

Rolling their blankets in a poncho after a night under the stars

Caring for animals

Awarding an honor

Outdoor council fire

Outdoor preparation of a meal

Y.W.C.A. girls playing volley ball

Camp Fire Girls taking part in the Thetford Pageant

Ready for a paddle in a war canoe

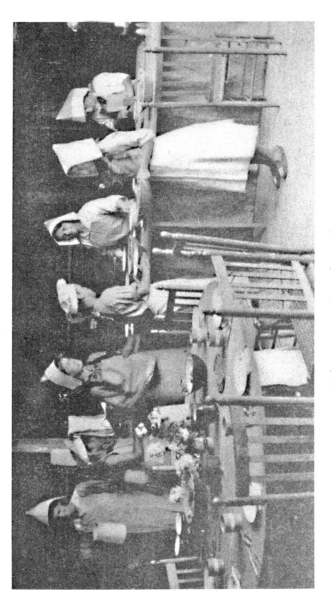

Indoor preparation of a meal

On a tramp

Making a silver bracelet. It is on the pitch block

Enjoying the picturesque while learning the art of paddling

Camp Fire Girls having an outing under the palisades. Ten cents each way and a mile and a half walk will give this wonderful sight to any girl of New York

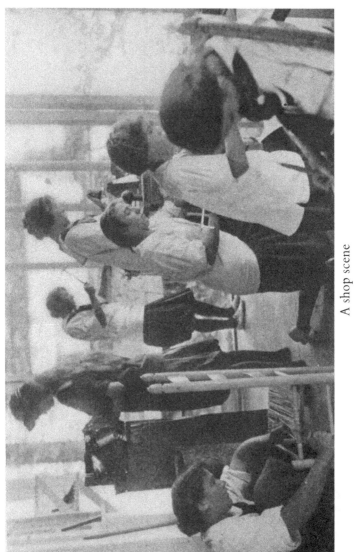

A shop scene

Sewing on dresses which have been designed and dyed to suit each girl

Making an angel dive

Helping to fight a real forest fire

Ceremonial head bands, bracelets, hatpins, rings and clasp pins

CPSIA information can be obtained
at www.ICGtesting.com
Printed in the USA
JSHW031348040322
23474JS00004B/16

9 781429 091039